Hey Sister, I'm Praying with You!

A 30-Day Interactive Prayer Devotional

Halaveshia S. Hall

Hey Sister, I'm Praying with You!

ISBN: 978-0-9994529-1-2
ISBN-13: 978-0-9994529-1-2

DEDICATION

I dedicate this book to the three beautiful souls the Creator allowed me carry and to care for during our time here on earth, the best bonus daughter one could ask for and the world's greatest nieces: Landon Laroy, Kaidynn Ilean, Bobby, Jr., Chassidy Loren, Patyence Jo & Aneesia Tasheem. Each of you are greatness walking and every breath you take is filled with perfection. Because you live, I will live forever.

In loving memory of my grandmother
Ruby Lee Morris respectfully known as "*Sister*"

Introduction

How many times have you been going through a storm or have been in a low place and you run across a family member, saint or a friend and the only thing they have to offer you is the overrated phrase of "I'm praying for you?" Besides the phrase "I love you" I believe "I'm praying for you" is the most over used, misused, feel-right-so-just say it statement ever mumbled by humanity. Like seriously, when someone utters the words "I am praying for you", I literally cringe. Mainly because I feel like if you are close enough to me to say you are praying for me you can STOP and pray WITH me. I feel the same way when someone strays away from the church and the saints say "Oh, just pray for So and So" No mam – No sir do not, I repeat DO NOT Pray for me – COME GET ME! I can feel my blood pressure rising as I type because this topic is such a sensitive topic for me. I believe we lose a lot of souls due to our lack of being proactive and hands-on in the Christian circuit.

We like to sit on our pews (or in our beautiful homes) in our comfort zones and send God to people instead of showing up with him. Well, not anymore! That behavior stops here, and I am starting with my sisters!! Sister, you are not in this alone and I will make sure you know this.

If you are in a bad place, we are going to pray and work you right out of it. Notice I said **pray** and **work** you right out of it? Why? Because James 2:26 (KJV) clearly states *So as the body without the spirit is dead, so faith without works is dead also.* Unfortunately, we do not just pray around here, we **WORK** or as I like to say to my sisters, we *Werk Sis! Ok!* Maybe, you're not in a bad place, did you know prayer is needed more in your good times than in your bad? My grandma, Ruby, would say "Keep some prayers up in your storehouse for those times when you won't be able to say a mumbling word!" AKA sis put you some prayers on lay-a-way. No matter what state you are in right now, I declare the next 30-days are about to be the best 30-days of your life. Get ready to build some things, break some things, open some doors, close some doors, create some doors and more importantly become the woman God designed you to be!
Are you ready?
Let's go, Sis!

CONTENTS

HEY SISTER!
I'M PROUD OF YOU - YOU'RE REALLY ABOUT TO START THIS JOURNEY!

I began this prayer journey:

_1_ day of _Aug_, 20_1_

I ended this prayer journey:

_____ day of _____, 20_____

After these 30-days I will:
(List 3-personal prayer goals)

1.

2.

3.

HEY SISTER!

This journey will not be easy, but I guarantee it will be worth it. Below are a few ways you can gain the best use of your new book and journey:

1. Join our continuous 30-day prayer calls by emailing info@mitlrevents.com to obtain the current schedule along with dial in information.

2. Gather a group of girlfriends and work through the 30-days together. Note: If you have a group of 10 or more you may reach out to author, Halaveshia S. Hall, invite her to join you on your 30th day and seal the deal with you. Contact her by logging on to www.halaveshiahall.com and completing the contact form.

3. Most importantly do the work or shall I say WERK SIS!

DAY 1

Peace

Oh, what a way to kick off our first day! Did you know the need for *peace* is universal and without it nothing seems to go right? Has *peace* been hard to obtain and maintain, for you? If so, let me ask you another question: Are you putting your quest for *peace* in the hands of God or in people? The holder and the source of your *peace* means a lot. It determines how long you have it. In God, his *peace* if sufficient and everlasting. In people, on the other hand, *peace* is subject to come and go.

Today's Prayer:
Dear God, I place my quest for *peace* in your hands, knowing you will provide me with *peace* that will surpass all understanding. I find comfort in knowing that your *peace* is sufficient and everlasting. I do not care how yesterday ended nor what today looks like, I am confident that my *peace* is here!

Today's Scriptures:
Philippians 4:7
Numbers 6:24-26
John 14:27

<u>YOUR WORK:</u>

Take control of your *peace* by identifying the following:
- ➤ What *peace* looks like to you.

- ➤ If you are not currently experiencing *peace*, identify why not.

- ➤ Begin the process of removing yourself from anything or anyone that strips you of or compromises your *peace* in any way.

Mediate a minimum 15 minutes.

Repeat as often as you need to.

What does *Peace* look like to me?

> Peace looks like no worries about things I can't control because I put everything in God's hands.

> Restful sleeping at night. Happy to wake up the next morning.

> Enjoying everyday/moment of life intentionally

Am I currently experiencing Peace? Why or Why Not?

To a certain extent
I am.
➤ I'm still working
through the pain I've
experienced.
➤ Also sorting out who
I am internally.

Hey Sister, I'm praying with you!
Today, I stand in agreement with
you and declare:
Your

Peace

is not on the way, it's already here!

DAY 2

Patience

Ok, today, I will tell on me first! *Patience* is not my strong suit. When they say "The struggle is real" um, yeah, the struggle is really real for me when it comes to this *patience* thing. But I am sure I am not the only one struggling with this and just in case I am not alone, I'd like to remind you that God's timing is perfect – like perfect Perfect! (Oh yeah, my daughter taught me that doubling my words makes it real). Do not allow an invisible biological clock, what's going on around you or what's happening for others, to discourage you and cause you to doubt God's perfect timing for your life. Beyond that, I have learned that im*patience* will land you into a lot of trouble that will take more time to get out of than having *patience* would have taken.

Today's Prayer:
Dear God, my prayer exceeds seeking *patience* as I would like your assistance with consistently walking in *patience*. It is my heart's desire to really walk out this *patience* thing, no matter how uncomfortable it may seem or how long my mind makes me feel something is taking to happen. Please give me a complete mind-shift so that I may embrace *patience.* I place my trust completely in you and trust your timing, no longer my timing.

Today's Scriptures:
Philippians 4:6
Ephesians 4:2
Galatians 6:9

14

YOUR WORK:

Begin to develop **patience** by identifying the following:

- ➤ The area(s) in your life you are struggling with having **patience.**

- ➤ How you can begin to practice **patience** in these areas, moving forward.

Mediate a minimum 15 minutes.

Repeat as often as you need to.

Werk Sis!

What area(s) of my life am I struggling with **Patience**?

> Patience in my job
> is im so eager for
> clients even those
> who aren't for me.

> Patience in friendship

> Patience in romance

How will I practice *Patience* in these areas, moving forward?

I will be slow to anger when it comes to dealing with clients, friends, and family.

I'm not perfect and people have patience with me.

Moving forward, I plan to have understanding before making any sudden emotional decisions.

Hey Sister, I'm praying with you!
Today, I stand in agreement with
you and declare:
Your

Patience

is not on the way, it's already here!

DAY 3

Strength

Ma'am, I sincerely hope you really know you are so much stronger than you think you are and if you do not, I pray you learn quickly. Sis, you are the epitome of **strength**. I mean, when you look in the dictionary your picture is sitting beside the word **strength**. If you don't believe me, stop and take a moment to reflect on ALL the things you've overcome just to get to today! In my Denzel Washington voice "King Kong ain't got nothing on you!" Sis, I really need you to understand that *right now* is so temporary! By this time next year, you will have forgotten why you were even feeling this way. You remember the last time, right? Look how you bounced back! Look at you still living! Chile, boo! **Strength** is your superpower!

Today's Prayer:
Dear God, please assist me in recognizing that YOU are my **strength** and because you are my **strength**; weakness, failing and giving up are not options. Continuously, bring to my memory that although I was created **strong**, I do not have to always be **strong** as I am **strong** in you and on my weakest day your **strength** prevails.

Today's Scriptures:
Philippians 4:13 ☑
Isaiah 40:29 & 31 ☑
Psalm 46:1 ☑

<u>YOUR WORK:</u>

Begin to develop *strength* by identifying the following:
- ➤ The things that cause you to feel like you do not have any *strength*.

Comparison, thinking of past

- ➤ Habits you can acquire to stand *strong* in those situations.

Self care & reading motivational

- ➤ Recognize when you do not have to be *strong* and you can fully depend on God to be *strong* for you.

Mediate a minimum 15 minutes.

Repeat as often as you need to.

Werk Sis!

What makes me feel like I do not have any **Strength?**

When I think about my faults and past mistakes.

When I think about my ex and the pain he put me through.

Depression & Worries

What can I do in these situations to stand **Strong?**

Read the Bible & do devotions
Stay connected in the Word.
Keep a guard out for
things that should stay
away from me.
Think about all I have
overcome in all that
I've accomplished.

Hey Sister, I'm praying with you!
Today, I stand in agreement with
you and declare:
Your

Strength

is not on the way, it's already here!

DAY 4

Restoration

Sis, you know what I love about God? Well, I love a lot of things about him, but there's this one thing that he does that blows my mind. He literally puts us back together again, and not in the same way but so much better than we were before.

In other words, his *restoration* skills are impeccable. Did you know that brokenness is not always a bad thing, and sometimes being broken is needed? If you thought you were "good" prior to your broken stage, sis, this *restoration* stage is going to completely blow your mind! Welcome to "Great"!

Today's Prayer:
Dear God, I pray for full *restoration* in every broken area of my life. I give you free reign to take my broken pieces and *restore* something great in me. I believe that you will *restore* everything better than it was before and I *THANK YOU* for my brokenness. Without being broken I would not have the ability to fully appreciate my complete *restoration*.

Today's Scriptures:
Isaiah 61:7
Job 42:10
1Peter 5:10

24

<u>YOUR WORK:</u>

Begin to prepare for your *restoration* by identifying the following:

> ➤ The area(s) in your life that require *restoration.*

> ➤ Actions you will take after you receive your *restoration* to show appreciation.

Clean up! Yes, I said clean up! Make room for the things that are about to be *restored.* How can you receive something you do not have room for? Here are a few examples:

> ➤ Expecting household/family *restoration*: Clean your home, remove excess clutter.
> ➤ Expecting financial *restoration*: Clean up your credit and begin to monitor your current spending habits.
> ➤ Expecting career *restoration*: Clean up your resume and/or your image.

Meditate a minimum of 15 minutes.

Repeat as often as you need to.

Werk Sis!

What areas of my life need *Restoration?*

What actions can I take after my *Restoration* to show appreciation for the things *restored*?

Hey Sister, I'm praying with you!
Today, I stand in agreement with
you and declare:
Your

Restoration

is not on the way, it's already here!

DAY 5

Power

Tell me a species, on earth, more *powerful* than a woman? I'll wait. There isn't one! Sis, as women, we are the most *powerful* beings ever created, but you knew that, right? I know you did. On top of being created *powerful*, we serve an all-*powerful* God and he resides within us. Can you say, double trouble? Make today the day you stop compromising and relinquishing your power.

Today's Prayer:
Dear God, please bring back to my remembrance just how *powerful* I am. Not only am I *powerful* in you but you created me *powerful*. Help me to understand the *power* I possess and the ability to walk in it unapologetically. I no longer want to give my *power* away.

Today's Scriptures:
2Timothy 1:7
Philippians 4:13
Ephesians 3:16

YOUR WORK:

Begin to regain your *power* by identifying the following:
- ➤ When you lost your *power.* Or who you lost your *power* to.

- ➤ Ways to get your *power* back and keep it.

Mediate a minimum 15 minutes.

Repeat as often as you need to.

Werk Sis!

When did I lose my *Power* or whom did I lose it to?

What are some ways I can regain my *Power?*

Hey Sister, I'm praying with you!
Today, I stand in agreement with
you and declare:
Your

Power

is not on the way, it's already here!

DAY 6

Worth

Pause! Re-read what we are focusing on, today. Read it aloud for the people in the back. It's a great day to discuss your **worth**. Why is it that we tend to forget how valuable we are? Like really, what happens that causes us to acquire amnesia when it pertains to our **worth**? I know! We tend to equate our worth to the misfortunes we've encountered; things like divorce, rape, miscarriages, failed friendships or absent parents. That's ok, we're about to change all of that, starting now. Today's a great day to determine your **worth** and add tax!!

Today's Prayer:

Dear God, today, I pray I not only remember my **worth**, but I'd also like the ability to unapologetically add tax to it, walk in it and own it. In you, I am fearfully and wonderfully made and there is no earthly value that can be placed on me – you paid the ultimate price for me, on the cross and I will no longer accept anything less than what I know I am **worth**!

Today's Scriptures:
Proverbs 31:10
Psalm 139:14
1Peter 2:9

YOUR WORK:

Begin to acknowledge your **worth** by identifying the following:

➤ What exactly does your **worth** look like to you, at this very moment (good or bad – write it out).

➤ If you are walking in the full potential of your **worth**. If not, why not?

Mediate a minimum 15 minutes.

Repeat as often as you need to.

What does my **Worth** look like to me? If it's good – let's make it better. If it's bad – let's work on raising your price.

Am I walking in the full potential of my God intended **Worth**? If not, what do I need to do?

Hey Sister, I'm praying with you!
Today, I stand in agreement with you and declare:
Your awareness and acceptance of your God intended

Worth

is not on the way, it's already here!

DAY 7

Beauty

SISTER! I must take a moment on this one because I need this one to sink in. Ma'am YOU ARE **_BEAUTIFUL_**! Do you even understand how **_beautiful_** you are? Stop right now, lay the book down well, wait carry the book with you, walk to a mirror and tell the very first person you see "Sis, you are the most **_beautiful_** person I have ever laid eyes on!" Every flaw you have makes you uniquely who you are and sister, that's **beautiful**. But you know what really makes you **_beautiful_**? Your heart, sis! That heart of yours is solid, even through pain, that heart of yours keeps right on living, right on loving, right on healing – WHEW CHILE – **_Beautiful_** is an understatement!!

Today's Prayer:
Dear God, I pray for complete revelation and acceptance of how **_beautiful_** I am from the inside out and the ability to stop comparing myself to others. Help me to accept everything about me the same way you do. Allow me to forget the things, words and/or people that have ever made me question my **_beauty_**.

Today's Scriptures:
1Peter 3:3-4
Ephesians 2:10
Proverbs 3:15

YOUR WORK:

Begin to fully accept your *beauty* by identifying the following:

➤ What *beauty* looks like to you, right now. (Good or Bad – write it out)

➤ Note all the things that make you feel *beautiful*.

Mediate a minimum 15 minutes.

Repeat as often as you need to.

Werk Sis!

What is my definition of *Beauty*?
(Do I currently feel *beautiful?*)

What makes me feel *Beautiful?*

Hey Sister, I'm praying with you!
Today, I stand in agreement with
you and declare:
Your awareness of your unique

Beauty

is not on the way, it's already here!

DAY 8

Favor

Listen! – *favor* ain't fair and it sure ain't free. Oh, but it is a mighty good day to be covered in *favor,* sis! It's not your fault God *favors* you. Just in case you are not aware of what *favor* is, let me remind you; it's those times when God placed you first when the world says you should have been last; it's that job you have that requires others to have a degree but for you – you just had to show up; oh yeah, it's that thing that happens when you just so happen to always be in the right place at the right time. Get it? Got it? Good! Last time I checked; you didn't ask for the *favor* on your life. I know I didn't! Stop apologizing for the *favor* God has bestowed upon you. He's God he does what he wants for who he wants. Point blank and a period!

Today's Prayer:
Dear God, *THANK YOU* for the abundant *favor* you have given me, the places you have taken me and the things you have done for me. When the world would say I am not qualified – you remind me that you do not call the qualified – you simply qualify the called! Help me to not only embrace my *favor* but also appreciate it.

Today's Scriptures:
Ephesians 1:11
Psalm 5:12
Proverbs 3:1-4

YOUR WORK:

Begin to show appreciation for the *favor* on your life by identifying the following:

> What *favor* looks like on your life.

> Specific times in your life God's *favor* has shown up for you. The times when you can truly say it was nobody *BUT GOD*.

Mediate a minimum 15 minutes.

Repeat as often as you need to.

Werk Sis!

What does the *Favor* on my life look like?

Provide a few examples of when you have seen God's *Favor* active in your life?

Hey Sister, I'm praying with you!
Today, I stand in agreement with
you and declare:
Your abundant

Favor

is not on the way, it's already here!

DAY 9

Love

Sister, you are the *love* that you seek and the *love* you desire is found only in God. But I am a realist, by DNA so, I know first hand that knowing this and living this out is so much easier said than done as we all desire to feel *love*, while here on earth from others. For that reason, it is my prayer that you become true, unconditional and unwavering *love* so that you may know it when you see it and receive it. This type of *love* comes by realizing how much *love* God has for you and mirror that, starting with how you *love* yourself then showing it to others.

Today's Prayer:
Dear God, show me what real *love* looks and feels like, in you. Allow me the opportunity to experience genuine, unconditional and unwavering *love* here on earth as well. More importantly, allow me to become the type of *love* I am seeking to my family, friends, companions and strangers.

Today's Scriptures:
1John 4:7-8
1Corithians 13:4-8
Romans 12:9-10

YOUR WORK:

Begin to recognize *love* by identifying the following:
- ➤ What *love* currently looks like to you.

- ➤ If you are displaying the *love* you are seeking.

Mediate a minimum 15 minutes.

Repeat as often as you need to.

Werk Sis!

What does **Love** look like to me?

Am I showing the *Love* I am looking for? If not, how can I began?

Hey Sister, I'm praying with you!
Today, I stand in agreement with you and declare:
Genuine, unconditional & unwavering

is not on the way, it's already here!

DAY 10

Faith

Sister Sister! Where is your *faith*? I know, perhaps, the same place mine is when things aren't going like I think they should be going; somewhere in lala land. Honestly, in bad situations, keeping the *faith* is the last thing I think about, but I have been making a conscious effort to end this pattern and you can too. Matter fact, we are going to start, today, sis! You with me? Let's go! One of the things I have been making a practice of doing is praising God in my bad times and in that alone, my *faith* has been growing and showing up tremendously. Wait, you do know that *faith* without work is dead, right? So, when we jump on this mega *faith* train we must do the work? Let's get to **Werk** Sis!!

Today's Prayer:

Dear God, please restore and/or increase my *faith*, in you. Help me to understand that I truly can do all things through you and just because I can't see you doesn't mean you're not working. Allow me to live in the peace of *delayed doesn't mean denied* and always remember when you move something you replace it with better. Help me to live every day in *faith* on purpose.

Today's Scriptures:
Hebrew 11:1 & 6
2Corinthians 5:7
Romans 10:17

YOUR WORK:

Begin to live every day in *faith,* on purpose, by identifying the following:

➢ Your current *faith* level.

➢ The area(s) in your life in which you can use a bit more *faith.*

Mediate a minimum 15 minutes.

Repeat as often as you need to.

Werk Sis!

Where is my current **Faith** level? Why?

What area in my life can I improve my **Faith**?

Hey Sister, I'm praying with you!
Today, I stand in agreement with
you and declare:
Your restored, increased and solid

Faith

is not on the way, it's already here!

DAY 11

Shine

Alexa play *Diamonds (***Shine*** Bright Like a Diamond)* by Rihanna and cue those huge Beyoncé fans while me and my sis, turn completely up! Oh, hey sis, excuse me, I have the tendency to get excited when I think about your glow! You're a light, darling, and beginning today, you will become completely un-dimmable (oh, by the way, I like making up words). Basically, after today, I pray you'll never dim your light again because it's unnecessary. The person beside you can either crank up their wattage or go to another room.

Today's Prayer:

Dear God, help me to understand that I was created to *shine* and dimming my light is no longer an option. On this journey, I realize, that I will never have to unscrew another woman's light in order to *shine* brighter nor will I have to dim my light to assist her in *shining* because you created us all to *shine* bright. As I *shine*, allow my light to reflect your will.

Today's Scriptures:
Matthew 5:14-16
Luke 11:33-36
Psalm 50:2

<u>YOUR WORK:</u>

Begin embracing your *shine* by identifying the following:
> ➤ If you are *shining* at your highest wattage.

> ➤ If you can *shine* brighter. If so, why aren't you?

Mediate a minimum 15 minutes.

Repeat as often as you need to.

Werk Sis!

Am I *Shining* at my highest wattage?

If not, why not? If so, is it possible for me to *Shine* brighter?

Hey Sister, I'm praying with you!
Today, I stand in agreement with
you and declare:
Your awareness of why you were created to

Shine

is not on the way, it's already here!

DAY 12

Smile

Smile sis – *smile* sis (inserts the old school cabbage patch dance with a mix of a southern Pentecostal shouting step)!! You're living your best life – despite what it looks like, believe me, you are living your best life and today's a great day to prove it. I declare that you will *smile* all day, today, even when you feel like crying sister girl, you better *smile*. Even a fake *smile* can eventually turn into laughter. You know why? Because your *smile* is beautiful, your *smile* is contagious, and your *smile* is your weapon.

Today's Prayer:
Dear God, it is my desire to genuinely *smile* and to live in peace while recognizing I am living the best days of my life. On the days I feel like I have nothing to *smile* about, help me to remember waking up is a reason alone to *smile* and carry on. It is my desire to rest in complete joy, in you. Joy, unlike happiness, gives me the ability to *smile* on my worst days.

Today's Scriptures:
Proverbs 15:30
Psalm 126:2-3
James 1:2-4

YOUR WORK:

Begin embracing your *smile* by identifying the following:
  ➢ The things that make you *smile*.

  ➢ When you do not feel like *smiling* what can you do *smile* on purpose

Today, as you practice *smiling* on purpose, take a little time to seek God for joy. I suggest you ask for joy over happiness. My god-father, Frederick Williams, Sr., taught me years ago that joy overrides happiness, as joy lives in you forever and always; whereas happiness based on circumstance and is subject to come and go. When you're grounded in joy you can *smile* more often.

Mediate a minimum 15 minutes.

Repeat as often as you need to.

What makes me to *Smile*?

What can I do to make sure I always **Smile**?

Hey Sister, I'm praying with you!
Today, I stand in agreement with
you and declare:
Your genuine and continuous

Smile

is not on the way, it's already here!

DAY 13

Dreams

Sis, let me ask you a question: Do you remember those *dreams* you had before life hit you? Those *dreams* you would write in your journal or day *dream* about all the time? Yes, life happened, things went left and somethings actually went right. You have found comfort and things seem to be working well, right now – that's cute, sis. But did you know until you take your last breath, the *dreams* you've placed on the shelf can still become reality. I mean, they may need a little adjusting now, to fit into what life has dealt you but today's a great day to remember those *dreams* and begin to work on how you can make them become reality. Whether you want to believe it or not, sis, you still have time.

Today's Prayer:
Dear God, please provide me with the insight and tools I need to breathe life back into the *dreams* I have somehow forgotten or allowed to die. Please restore my passion for the things I have always desired to do and/or become. Thank you for allowing life to happen as it has strengthened me and prepared me to live out my full potential, through you.

Today's Scriptures:
Philippians 4:13
Proverbs 16:3
Matthew 6:33

<u>YOUR WORK</u>:

Begin to revive your **dreams** by identifying the following:

➢ What **dreams** have you placed on the shelf or allowed to die that you would like to see become a reality.

➢ The steps you can begin to take to work towards fulfilling your **dreams**.

Mediate a minimum 15 minutes.

Repeat as often as you need to.

Werk Sis!

What are some *Dreams* I've placed on a shelf or allowed to die?

What steps can I take towards making my *Dreams* a reality?

Hey Sister, I'm praying with you!
Today, I stand in agreement with
you and declare:
The rebirth and full execution of your

Dreams

is not on the way, it's already here!

DAY 14

Forward

Sis, I pray you only look back to use it as fuel to PUSH *FORWARD*. *Forward* motion looks great on you. One of the best things you can do is release your past along with the people, memories and things that try to hold you there. It's perfectly ok to remember things but the only reason you remember parts of your past is to serve as a reminder for you to never go back and use the memories as fuel to move ahead.

Today's Prayer:
Dear God, help me to move *forward* with no regrets of genuinely forgetting those things behind me. I am aware that in you all things are made new and I declare *I am a new person* and nothing behind me matters. God, today, I *THANK YOU* for my new beginning and fresh start.

Today's Scriptures:
Philippians 3:12-14

<u>YOUR WORK</u>:

Begin to finally move completely *forward* by identifying the following:

> ➤ What moving *forward* looks like to you.

> ➤ What is keeping you from moving *forward*. Once you figure this out – let it go!

> ➤ The steps you need to take to move *forward* and not look back.

Mediate a minimum 15 minutes.

Repeat as often as you need to.

Werk Sis!

What does moving *Forward* look like to me?

What is stopping me from moving *Forward?*
(What are some things I am holding on to that I need to let go?)

Hey Sister, I'm praying with you!
Today, I stand in agreement with
you and declare:
Your ability to let go and move

Forward

is not on the way, it's already here!

DAY 15

Purpose

It's a marvelous day to define your *purpose* or at least come close. How much longer do you plan on walking around unsure of why you are really here? Finding your *purpose* isn't as hard as you may think it is. It can really be as simple as asking God what your *purpose* is and accepting it when it's revealed. When you realize what it is, you'll feel like that person that lost their cell phone while it was in their hand or the person that looked for their glasses while wearing them. Yep, that's how close your *purpose* is to you. Take some time and tap into your *purpose*, today.

Today's Prayer:
Dear God, please reveal my *purpose* to me and help me to understand it. I know you created me to be more than who I am, right now. Help me to realize that my *purpose* looks nothing like someone else's *purpose* so to look at others and become discouraged is not your will. I have my own unique *purpose* and today, I'd like you to reveal it to me.

Today's Scriptures:
Jeremiah 29:11
Proverbs 19:21
Ephesians 2:10

YOUR WORK:

Begin defining your **purpose** by identifying the following:
> What you believe your **purpose** is.

> After spending some time with God, if his definition of your **purpose** and your definition of your **purpose** align.

Mediate a minimum 15 minutes.

Repeat as often as you need to.

My *Purpose* looks like:

God confirmed my *Purpose* is:

Hey Sister, I'm praying with you!
Today, I stand in agreement with
you and declare:
The revelation of your

Purpose

is not on the way, it's already here!

DAY 16

You

What a magnificent day to be authentically *YOU*! Besides, everyone else is taken. *You* are a rare breed and as a matter of fact, *you* are the only one of *YOU*. Even identical twins are uniquely different and that alone is enough to be proud of. I truly pray *you* unapologetically accept who *you* are. No regrets. No second guessing. No worries. No comparisons. Love on *yourself*, today just because.

Today's Prayer:

Dear God, please allow me to accept who I authentically am. I apologize for ever thinking I wanted to be like someone else or comparing myself to anyone else. Today, I chose to embrace me and every flaw that comes along with me. I am assured that when you created me, you purposely set me apart and created me differently. You took extra time to perfectly create my imperfections and I *THANK YOU*.

Today's Scriptures:
Galatians 1:10
1Corinthians 11:1
Psalm 139:14

<u>YOUR WORK:</u>

Begin embracing the unique person *you* are by identifying the following:

➤ The things you love about *yourself.*

➤ The qualities *you* have that set you apart from others. Once you figure these out –embrace them!

Mediate a minimum 15 minutes.

Repeat as often as you need to.

Things that I love about being me.

My unique qualities that set me apart from others.

Hey Sister, I'm praying with you!
Today, I stand in agreement with
you and declare:
Your true acceptance of

You

is not on the way, it's already here!

DAY 17

Trust

Today, we are snatching Band-Aids off. Sorry sis, but we must dive a little deep on this one. ***Trust*** issues are common, and they cut deep. The saying: *The most expensive thing in the world is **trust**; it can take years to earn and just a matter of seconds to lose* is so true. After your ***trust*** is compromised ***trusting*** anyone about anything becomes a full-time job within itself. My heart aches when we lose ***trust*** in God based on what someone else has done to us. So, today, sis, I am praying that God completely restores your ***trust***. Be it your ***trust*** in him, your fellow sister/brother, church, personal or work relationships, etc. Whatever area in which you have fallen short of ***trust*** he's going to restore it.

Today's Prayer:

Dear God, it is my desire that you restore my ***trust***, especially my ***trust*** in you. True, I have reasons to never ***trust*** again, but I refuse to live my life in that box and because of you, I do not have to. Help me to genuinely put my ***trust*** in you, allowing you to guard my heart and reveal to me whom I should ***trust***. Take away that part of me that automatically loses my ***trust*** in you after I am hurt by others. There are so many relationships I desire to make workout, but I am afraid to ***trust***, that ends today as the spirit of fear is not your will.

Today's Scriptures:
Joshua 1:9
Psalm 9:10
Proverbs 3:5-6

YOUR WORK:

Begin reclaiming your *trust* by identifying the following:
- ➤ The area(s) in your life where there is room for more *trust*.

- ➤ Why you lost *trust* in those areas to begin with.

- ➤ What you can do, moving forward, to maintain your *trust* in God.

Mediate a minimum 15 minutes.

Repeat as often as you need to.

Werk Sis!

What area(s) in my life do I have room for more *Trust?* Why did I lose *Trust* in the first place?

Steps I can take to keep my *Trust* in God.

Hey Sister, I'm praying with you!
Today, I stand in agreement with
you and declare:
Your ability to

Trust

is not on the way, it's already here!

DAY 18

Health

How's your *health* looking, sis? I am not only asking about your physique, as I believe in total *health*: mind, body and spirit. It is God's will for us to be *healthy* in all areas of our lives. How's your mental *health*, sis? Are you aware that God agrees with counseling? If you are having any mental issues, depression, low moments or the feeling of being all alone it's perfectly okay to seek counseling from a trained therapist. While having faith, praying and attending church is awesome there are times when we need to seek a little more help. The same way you'd reach out to a personal trainer or dietician for your physical *health*, understood? Good. How's your physical *health*? You know you can't be a champion out here in these Godly streets with high blood pressure, obese or purposely ignoring your physical *health*. Things beyond your control are understandable but if you can control it – let's fix it, sis? Ok? Oh, what about your spiritual *health*? Did you know that spending time with God and reading your word, daily is a form of exercise for your spirit?

Today's Prayer:
Dear God, I am aware that it is your desire for me to be *healthy* in all areas of my life. Please assist me with living that out. If I am experiencing any issues, I ask for complete restoration, the ability to seek help and if it's anything within my control, please grant me the wisdom and resources to fix it.

Today's Scriptures:
1Corithians 6:19-20
3John 1:2
Jeremiah 33:6

YOUR WORK:

Begin prioritizing your *health* by identifying the following:

➢ If you have any *health* (physical, spiritual or mental) issues. If so, identify if they are beyond your control or are they things you can control.

➢ How much of a priority have you placed on your *health* (physical, spiritual and mental) in the past.

Mediate a minimum 15 minutes.

Repeat as often as you need to.

What is the current state of my mental, physical and spiritual *Health?*

If I have any **Health** issues are they beyond my control / something
I can control and seek help for?

Hey Sister, I'm praying with you!
Today, I stand in agreement with
you and declare:
Your renewed and/ or continued great

Health

is not on the way, it's already here!

DAY 19

Family

Sis, if you are anything like me, you love your *family* even when you don't like them. (You'll catch that later) *Family* can be a hand full and can cause you to lose a few pounds, nights of sleep and your edges but there's nothing we wouldn't do for them. Today, is a great day to pray for covering and closeness of your *family*. No matter how you want to spin it and what things may look like after a not-so good *family* gathering – *family* is everything and should always come first. I have witnessed a lot of people on a mission to save the world while leaving their *family* behind. This shouldn't be. I'm clear some people do not want to be helped but most times I find it, as habit, due to past situations, we jump to save the world and walk right past our *family*. Then, there are those moments when we should turn some *family* members over to God, but we wear ourselves down holding on to and trying to fix them. Today, is all about *family*.

Today's Prayer:
Dear God, when speaking on *family*, the serenity prayer is a great place to start. It is my heart's desire that you continuously cover my *family* (immediate and far) in all areas of their lives and bring us closer. Help me to identify the *family* members that I can assist and those that I need to hand over to you, completely. *THANK YOU* for my *family*, the good the bad and the ugly. I appreciate my *family*.

Today's Scriptures:
1Timothy 5:8
Colossians 3:13
1Corithians 13:4-7

<u>YOUR WORK:</u>

Embrace your *family* by identifying the following:
> ➢ If there is room for you to be closer to your *family*.
> If there is room work on filling that room.

> ➢ What *family* looks like to you.

Mediate a minimum 15 minutes.

Repeat as often as you need to.

Werk Sis!

Do I have any room to become closer to my *Family*? If so, what are some ways I can start to become closer?

What does *Family* look like to me?

Hey Sister, I'm praying with you!
Today, I stand in agreement with
you and declare:
*God's covering, continued protection and
closeness of your*

Family

is not on the way, it's already here!

DAY 20

Finances

If you have ever attended one of my *Meeting in the Ladies Room Women Seminars* you already know how I feel about your *finances*, sis and if you don't know, let me fill you in really quick. You can have every bit of faith, prayer life on fleek, the love of your life, an amazing job and great health but if your *finances* are jacked up - I'm sorry to tell you sis, you are jacked up. Bad *finances* and awful stewardship over what God provides places you in a terrible place. Eventually, that good ole faith you have will diminish, your prayer life will begin to look more like begging and frustration, the love of your life will become your enemy, the job will begin to feel like a prison and due to worrying all areas of your health will soon decline. Trust me on this one. You can't function with jacked up *finances*. Today's a great day to get your affairs in order. It may take some time but hey, starting is half the battle.

Today's Prayer:
Dear God, teach me to be a great steward over my *finances*. Control any impulses I may have that will cause me to jeopardize my *finances*. I realize, it is not your will that I live pay check to pay check or month to month

Today's Scriptures:
John 15:4-5
Matthew 6:31-33
Proverbs 13:22

YOUR WORK:

Begin taking control of your **finances** by identifying the following:

> - Area(s) you have room for improvement your **finances**.

> - Three **financial** goals you would like to reach by the end of the year.

Mediate a minimum 15 minutes.

Repeat as often as you need to.

What areas do I have room for improvement in my *Finances?*

What are three *Financial* goals I would like to reach by the end of the year?

Hey Sister, I'm praying with you!
Today, I stand in agreement with
you and declare:
A complete increase and stability in your

Finances

is not on the way, it's already here!

DAY 21

Success

Start today off by defining what *success* looks like for you. Not what social media has defined it to be or what your friend's *success* looks like; but honestly ask yourself, what does *success* look like to you. Whatever it looks like I am praying you *succeed* in it. When it comes to your *success*, I need you to know that you deserve it. My sister-friend, Jill, called me out a few weeks ago by saying "You constantly shrink when it comes to embracing your *success* and being *successful*, why?" She pointed out instances that I have literally ran from *success*. Wow! Is all I could say. If this is you, today, sis, we are praying the exact same prayer.

Today's Prayer:
Dear God, help me to embrace my *success* as it's your will that I *succeed* in all areas of my life. Reveal to me ways to stop shrinking. It is my heart's desire to be *successful*, through you, in all things I set out to do. While failure is not an option neither is shrinking.

Today's Scriptures:
Philippians 4:13
Luke 16:10-11
Proverbs 16:3

YOUR WORK:

Begin embracing your *success* by identifying the following:

> ➤ Your definition of *success*.

> ➤ If you consider yourself *successful*.

Mediate a minimum 15 minutes.

Repeat as often as you need to.

Werk Sis!

My definition of *Success*.

Do I consider myself *Successful?*

Hey Sister, I'm praying with you!
Today, I stand in agreement with
you and declare:
Your continuous and steady

Success

is not on the way, it's already here!

DAY 22

Gifts

It's a fact sis, your *gifts* (also known as talent) will make room for you in all areas of your life. Today's a great day to identify those *gifts* and acknowledge if you are utilizing them to your fullest potential. We tend to block our own blessings by sitting on the things we have been freely given. Have you noticed that most successful people are only doing things they were *gifted* to do that they love and in return they are being paid for it? That's what the making room part does.

Today's Prayer:
Dear God, *THANK YOU* for the *gifts* you have given me. Please assist me in identifying and utilizing every *gift* you have given me. It is my heart's desire to no longer sit on these *gifts* but to share them with the world, as you intended.

Today's Scriptures:
1Peter 4:10-11
1Corinthians 4:4-6
Hebrew 2:3-5

<u>YOUR WORK:</u>

Begin embracing your *gifts* by identifying the following:
➢ Exactly what your *gifts* are.

➢ If you are utilizing all your *gifts*. If not, why not.

Mediate a minimum 15 minutes.

Repeat as often as you need to.

What are my *Gifts*?

Am I utilizing all my *Gifts*? If not, why not?

Hey Sister, I'm praying with you!
Today, I stand in agreement with
you and declare:
*Complete utilization and God ordained
room for your*

Gifts

is not on the way, it's already here!

DAY 23

Motivation

Today's a great day to be *motivated* and to *motivate*. Sis, I'm very aware that staying *motivated* is a job within itself let alone the constant ability to *motivate* others. Sometimes, we barely want to get out of bed. But it's our due diligence to spread joy and what better way than through *motivating* the next person? You'll find that in *motivating* someone else you'll begin to *motivate* yourself. Try it and let me know how it goes.

Today's Prayer:
Dear God, as I am *motivated*, allow me to *motivate* others. On the days I feel *motivation* is as far from me as the sun is from the earth, bring back to my remembrance your greatness that in turn *motivates* me. It's my heart's desire to constantly be *motivated* to become a better me.

Today's Scriptures:
Matthew 17:20
2Timothy 1:7
2Corinthians 4:1

<u>YOUR WORK:</u>

Start a daily regime of *motivation* by identifying the following:

> ➢ What *motivates* you.

> ➢ What you can do to *motivate* others.

Mediate a minimum 15 minutes.

Repeat as often as you need to.

Werk Sis!

What *Motivates* me?

What can I do to *Motivate* others?

Hey Sister, I'm praying with you!
Today, I stand in agreement with
you and declare:
Continuous

Motivation

is not on the way, it's already here!

DAY 24

P.U.S.H.

Ahhhh yes, the infamous P.U.S.H. – *Pray Until Something Happens.* Yep, that's what we are doing, today! We are praying until the heavens move on our behalf. But you know I can't just have you out here in these streets praying and stressing, sis, we are also doing the work, today, to make something happen. If it's within our power to physically **PUSH** through that's what we are doing, today.

Today's Prayer:
Dear God, please grant me the ability to identify the things that I have control of and that I can **PUSH** through. I understand the power of prayer and I also understand the power of adding work to prayer and faith. I'm tired of being stuck where I am, and I know it's not your desire that I am stagnant. Show me what to do to move past this and **PUSH** through to my breakthrough.

Today's Scriptures:
Jeremiah 32:27
Isaiah 62:1-3
Matthew 7:7

YOUR WORK:

Prepare to *P.U.SH.* through by identifying the following:
- ➤ Where you're stuck at / what you're stuck on which in return will uncover what you need to *P.U.S.H.* through.

- ➤ What *P.U.S.H.*ing through looks like to you.

Mediate a minimum 15 minutes.

Repeat as often as you need to.

Werk Sis!

What do I need to P.U.S.H. through?

What does **P.U.S.H.**ing through looks like to me?

Hey Sister, I'm praying with you!
Today, I stand in agreement with
you and declare:
Your ability to always

P.U.S.H

is not on the way, it's already here!

DAY 25

Praise

No matter what yesterday looked like or how today is beginning to start out – put a *praise* in your mouth and begin to *praise* God, just because! Oh, yeah, that's all we are doing today, *praising* God. Need a few reminders of why you should be *praising*? Let's start with an over view of all the things he's done for you. That's not enough? Well, let's reflect on the fact you didn't have to be here, today, but you're here. I think that's enough encouraging, at least it did it for me – let me stop and take a *praise* break! I'll meet you in *praise*.

Today's Prayer:
Dear God, my only desire, today, is to *praise* your name because you are worthy to be *praised*. I have no requests; only *praise*!

Today's Scriptures:
Psalm 146:1-2
Psalm 150:3-5
2Samuel 22:4

YOUR WORK:

Praise God – on Purpose
ALL DAY!

Repeat as often as you need to.

Werk Sis!

Reasons I am giving God *Praise*?

More reasons I am giving God *Praise*?

Hey Sister, I'm praying with you!
Today, I stand in agreement with
you and declare:
Your never-ending

Praise

is not on the way, it's already here!

DAY 26

Grace

God's *grace* is enough and incomparable. Today's a great day to acknowledge the *grace* that's on your life. *Grace* is often defined as *unmerited favor* or God's goodness towards us for no apparent reason. Yes, something that he chooses to do. Another way to identify *grace* is the mere fact *we are saved by grace* meaning we have received salvation as an extraordinary expression of God's *grace* not based on our works or anything that we have done. Now, you may be wondering what's the difference between *grace* and favor – simply put – *grace* is a form of favor that we should never take for granted. A better way to view it is to always remember the phrase: *he didn't have to do it but he did!*

Today's Prayer:
Dear God, please help me to identify your sufficient and incomparable *grace* on my life. Please help me with my lack of acknowledging your *grace* or acknowledging when you didn't have to do something but you did.

Today's Scriptures:
2Corinthians 12:8-9
Romans 3:20-24
Ephesians 4:7

YOUR WORK:

Begin accepting your *grace* by identifying the following:

➤ Instances you've witnessed God's *grace* in your life.

➤ Your definition of *grace*.

Mediate a minimum 15 minutes.

Repeat as often as you need to.

Werk Sis!

Instances when I have witnessed God's *Grace* at work in my life.

My definition of *Grace*?

Hey Sister, I'm praying with you!
Today, I stand in agreement with
you and declare:
God's infinite and sufficient

Grace

is not on the way, it's already here!

DAY 27

Humility

One of the best characteristics you can possess is the characteristic of **humility**. Sis, to remain **humble**, in all things is a gift within itself. Today's a great day to go before God and request an extra dose of **humility**. Even if you have an ample supply, you can always use more.

Today's Prayer:
Dear God, to remain **humble**, is a direct requirement from you to me and I'd like to walk in it daily. Touch my heart and renew my mind to allow me to always remain **humble**.

Today's Scriptures:
1Peter 5:6-7
Colossians 3:12-14
Ephesians 4:2
Philippians 2:3-11

YOUR WORK:

Begin growing in *humility* by identifying the following:
- ➤ What *humility* means to you.

- ➤ Areas you can improve in remaining *humble*.

Mediate a minimum 15 minutes.

Repeat as often as you need to.

What is my definition of *Humility*?

Areas I can improve in remaining *Humble:*

Hey Sister, I'm praying with you!
Today, I stand in agreement with
you and declare:
Your ability to always walk in

Humility

is not on the way, it's already here!

DAY 28

Grateful

How do you show **gratitude**? How often do you show **gratitude**? How many times a day do you express to God and others how **grateful** you are? Well, today's a great day to start expressing **gratitude** or either began to express it more. I totally get how we can become so consumed with the everyday antics of life and forget to say *THANK YOU*; not only to God but those that mean something to us as well.

Today's Prayer:
Dear God, *THANK YOU*!

Today's Scriptures:
1Chronicles 16:34
1Thessolonians 5:18
Psalm 100:1-5

<u>YOUR WORK:</u>

Express your *gratitude* by identifying the following:

➢ Identify some people you'd like to express your *gratitude* for. Once you identify them – contact them and express your *gratitude*.

➢ List several things you are *grateful* for.

Mediate a minimum 15 minutes.

Repeat as often as you need to.

Who do I need to reach out to and let them know I am *Grateful* for them?

My *Gratitude* list:

Hey Sister, I'm praying with you!
Today, I stand in agreement with
you and declare:
Your ability to remain

Grateful

is not on the way, it's already here!

DAY 29

Time for You

Sis, listen, self-care is the best care and we all know this; but why it is so hard to follow through with this? Did you know: You can be a great mother and take *time for yourself*. You can be an amazing wife and still *take time for yourself*. You can be the best employee in the world and still *take time for yourself*. I promise you, it's possible and nothing will break while you are indulging in mandatory "*me time*". Yes, I said, mandatory because if you do not take time to take care of yourself you will become useless to those around you. You can't properly care for, assist, love, appreciate or effectively do any of the other things you do for others without first, doing them for yourself. Today's a great day to try it out.

Today's Prayer:
Dear God, help me to find peace in *taking care of me*. It is not your will that I only exist in this world; but your desire is that I live out my fullest potential and that's something I cannot do if I am not properly taking care of myself and *taking time for me*.

Today's Scriptures:
Mark 6:31-32
Mark 1:35
1Corinthians 6:19-20

YOUR WORK:

Begin creating *time for you* by identifying the following:
- ➤ The last time you made *time for you*.

- ➤ Time you can set aside to MAKE *time for you*.

Mediate a minimum 15 minutes.

Repeat as often as you need to.

Werk Sis!

When was the last time I made *Time for me?*

What times can I set aside to MAKE *Time for me?*

Hey Sister, I'm praying with you!
Today, I stand in agreement with
you and declare:
*Your ability to make a conscious effort to
always make*

Time for You

is not on the way, it's already here!

DAY 30

Sisters

On this final day, it is my desire that you take time to pray with your *sisters* on a regular basis. I'd like for you to realize that your *sister* may not be someone your mother birthed but she is every female of every race, nationality, financial bracket and background. Collectively, we can do so much. Separately, we are nothing. Today's a great day to reach out to your *sisters* if only to say "Sis, I love you". When you say "I am my *sister's* keeper" mean it and act on it. Don't become the woman you despise; meaning, you know how it feels to be shunned or left out, to be an outcast or not included in things and looked down upon by other women. Don't be that chick, sis!

Today's Prayer:
Dear God, *THANK YOU* for my *sisters* as they reflect me. Remove any ounce of competition I may have in my body as it is your will that we connect and not compete. Help me to acknowledge the great works my *sisters* are doing and the ability to be vulnerable and open with my *sisters*. Remove the shame of transparency so that I may connect with my *sisters* on the realest level possible.

Today's Scriptures:
James 4:11
Ecclesiastics 4:9-10
James 2:14-17

YOUR WORK:

Begin building your interactive circle of **sisters** by identifying the following:

➤ A list of **sisters** you'd like to connect with, pray with and constantly check on.

➤ A timeframe you plan on connecting with these **sisters**.

Mediate a minimum 15 minutes.

Repeat as often as you need to.

My circle of *Sisters*:

Date(s) I plan on connecting with these *Sisters*:

Hey Sister, I'm praying with you!
Today, I stand in agreement with
you and declare:
*Your passion to always stop & assist,
motivate, encourage, uplift, cover and most
importantly, pray with your fellow*

Sisters

is not on the way, it's already here!

ACKNOWLEDGEMENTS

To my parents:

My mother, Agnes Morris, you did everything you knew how to do to raise me and I appreciate you for it. You are the reason I am the strong and independent woman I am today. You have the most beautiful smile I have ever seen, and it has always brightened my day, it is my prayer that you genuinely smile more often.

My biological father, Willie C. Hall, may you forever rest in peace and know that every day, I strive to live a life that makes you proud. Thank you for doing your service on this earth.

My God-sent parents, LeRoy & Helen Davis, Sr., "Thank You" is not good enough for everything you both provided for me and instilled in me. Please know that I will forever love you.

My uncle-dad and aunt-mom, Darryl & Kawanda Hines, Sr., you stepped in when others walked away and declared that in spite of my circumstances, I would have no excuse to be the BEST ME that I could be and I thank you for that. You opened your home and hearts to me when I had nowhere to go.

My spiritual parents, Frederick & Felicia Williams, Sr., I will forever be grateful for the knowledge and the covering you both have provided for me all these years. Even when I am not around physically, you keep me lifted in spirit. I will love you forever.

To my siblings:

Joseph, Fredrick, Jacqueline, Aaron, Donuell, Willie, Phillip, LeRoy, Jr., Kerry, Frederick, Jr., Victoria, Vanessa, Fredesha, Natasha, Lawanna, and Nazarell I love you and I am proud to be your sister. Tanzineka you define "sister-cousin"! Josh you define "brother-cousin" Shanda, Jill & Kenisha you three define when friends exceed friendship and turn family! #SisterSisters

To my family and friends:

Extremely too many to name but know that this is for the descendants of Rosa C. Sanders, Ruby L. Morris, Jessie Williams, Alice Brown & Bill Lane. Where would I be without you? Thank you for all your continued support and love.

To my corporate sisters:

Lisa, Gwenetta, Muriel, Kim, Seniqua and Ronada it's very rare that a person can take a corporate relationship to a personal level, but you ladies stepped into my life on the corporate circuit and changed my life, forever. Thank you for taking the time to mentor, help and groom me inside and outside of the corporate world and beyond that, I thank you for being a friend.

To my Turner Chapel AME Church (TCC) family:

Thank you for being a safe haven and an example of God's will, here on earth. You exemplify the true meaning of kingdom people as you are not just a church building, you are the church living. A solid pillar in the community for over 150 years. The women of TCC exemplify the true meaning of sisterhood and take the phrase *I am my sister's keeper* serious and I appreciate you all.

To my spiritual sisters:

Young, old, rich, poor, black, white or in between – I LOVE YOU! Without us, the world would not exist.
We are WOMEN – We are FABULOUS – We are SISTERS
#IamMySistersKeeper

Auntie I told you about this book for the last two years and you were super excited to see it manifest. Unfortunately, God needed you with him before I could physically deliver you a copy. Thank you for your encouragement and constant support. It's here, sugar mama, I did the work!
Mary Jackson Foster
Oct. 1946~Mar. 2019

ABOUT THE AUTHOR

Halaveshia S. Hall is a native of Albany, Ga. She is the mother of three biological children and one bonus daughter. Motivational Speaker and co-founder of *A Meeting in the Ladies Room Women Seminars* (MITLRWS) her passion to assist in enhancing the lives of all women is a priority. Each seminar includes financial education, new speaker platforms, image literacy, small business creation education, mental health awareness, membership to a virtual book club and much more to help today's woman flourish.

Connect with Halaveshia on Facebook and Instagram @Halaveshia and www.halaveshiahall.com
Connect with MITLRWS via www.mitlrevents.com

Follow "Hey Sister!" books via Instagram @heyheysisters

61710683R00089

Made in the USA
Columbia, SC
29 June 2019